LEADERSHIP KEYS
FIELD GUIDE

LEADERSHIP KEYS FIELD GUIDE

Emotional Intelligence Tools for Great Leadership

by

Reldan S. Nadler, Psy.D.

PSYCCESS
PRESS

Santa Barbara, CA

A Division of True North Leadership, Inc.
1170 Camino Meleno
Santa Barbara, CA 93111
805-683-1066
Fax 805-692-6738
www.truenorthleadership.com

A Division of True North Leadership, Inc.
1170 Camino Meleno
Santa Barbara, CA 93111
805-683-1066, Fax 805-692-6738
www.truenorthleadership.com

Printed in Canada.

Publisher's Cataloging-In-Publication

Nadler, Reldan S., 1951-

    Leadership keys field guide: emotional intelligence tools for great leadership / by Reldan S. Nadler. — Santa Barbara, CA : Psyccess Press, 2007.

       p. ; cm.

       ISBN-13: 978-0-9759744-3-9
       ISBN-10: 0-9759477-3-7
       Includes bibliographical references.

       1. Leadership. 2. Emotional intelligence. 3. Personnel management. I. Title.

HD57.7 .N334 2007
658.4/092—dc22   CIP

Cover and Book Designer: Patricia Bacall
Author Photograph: Juli Hayes
Editor: Ilene Segalove
Copyeditor: Brookes Nohlgren
Book Consultant: Ellen Reid

CONTENTS

INTRODUCTION

Leadership Keys is a desk reference of easy-to-use tools, skills, and actions designed to immediately raise your Emotional Intelligence (EI) and create more Star Performers in your organization. People who possess high Emotional Intelligence succeed at work (performing in the top 10 percent), build flourishing careers, cultivate long-lasting relationships, and create a balanced work/home life.

This field guide offers extra information and support to help you use the Keys and get a jump-start on raising your Emotional Intelligence. Get ready to practice and perform these simple tools to turn your leadership and your teams from good to great!

> *People who possess high Emotional Intelligence succeed at work (performing in the top 10 percent), build flourishing careers, cultivate long-lasting relationships, and create a balanced work/home life.*

WHAT IS
EMOTIONAL INTELLIGENCE?

Emotional Intelligence means exhibiting a good balance of personal and social competencies in the following four distinct areas of behavior and leadership:

1. Self-Awareness—Understanding yourself
2. Self-Management—Managing yourself
3. Social Awareness—Understanding others
4. Relationship Management—Managing others

Below are the 20 competencies presented by the authors Cherniss and Goleman in *The Emotionally Intelligent Workplace.*[1] To be a Star Performer, you do not have to excel in every competency inside of each of the four areas. Your goal, instead, is to develop a good balance across the board. Note that the competencies you see in **BOLD** are featured in the Leadership Keys.

THE 4 AREAS AND 20 COMPETENCIES OF EMOTIONAL INTELLIGENCE

PERSONAL	SOCIAL
Self-Awareness	**Social Awareness**
Emotional Self-Awareness	**Empathy**
Accurate Self-Assessment	Organizational Awareness
Self-Confidence	Service Orientation
Self-Management	**Relationship Management**
Emotional Self-Control	**Influence**
Trustworthiness	**Inspirational Leadership**
Conscientiousness	**Developing Others**
Adaptability	**Building Bonds**
Achievement Orientation	**Teamwork and Collaboration**
Initiative	**Conflict Management**
	Communication
	Change Catalyst

(Cherniss and Goleman, 2001)[2]

MICRO-INITIATIVES CREATE MACRO-IMPACT

Leadership Keys make it simple to help you understand and review how to raise your Emotional Intelligence. If you take the initiative and only do a few things differently, you will separate yourself from the average pack and propel yourself to star status. Keep the Keys nearby, on your desk or in your briefcase. Use them regularly, one at a time or in combination, as a reference to inspire, inform, and boost your daily performance. Make sure to review your Keys for a few minutes prior to a meeting or leadership initiative and you'll see how micro-initiatives create macro-impact.

WHO SHOULD USE THE KEYS?

No matter who you are, you or your direct reports will benefit from implementing these Keys.

1. Are you a leader, manager, supervisor, or team leader? If so, distribute the Keys to everyone on your team so that all of you use the same tools and speak the same language.

2. Are you a coach, trainer, or consultant? Then give the Keys to the leaders and clients you work with to reinforce your coaching and keep your clients accountable and growing.

WHEN TO USE THE KEYS

Refer to your Keys when you:

- Speak to your team or clients about where they are going
- Wish to hold accountability or acknowledge performance
- Delegate a task
- Give feedback to an employee or co-worker
- Coach an employee to better performance
- Make a presentation or mediate a conflict
- Lose control and need to manage your emotions
- Decide what level of involvement you want from your team on a decision
- Deal with your boss or partner
- Give a talk to ensure you are not misunderstood

HOW TO USE THE KEYS

Once you choose which Key you need today, review the card and then locate the Key #1–10 in this field guide to find out more about:

- When to use the Key
- Unlocking the Key—what is the concept behind the Key
- Key anecdotal examples
- Practicing the Key

WHY IMPROVE YOUR EI?

The higher up you are in an organization, the more Emotional Intelligence, versus intelligence or technical expertise, determines your leadership success, contributing as much as 85-90 percent.[3]

- Leaders high in Emotional Intelligence are more productive.[4]

- Great leaders also have a positive impact on profitability, turnover, employee commitment, customer satisfaction, and retention.[5]

- The more great leaders an organization develops, the more it will become an outstanding organization.[6]

- Emotions are contagious. As a top leader, you influence the whole climate of your team as much as 50-70 percent.[7]

- Gallup has found that if U.S. workers were 5 percent more engaged, it would boost national productivity by $79 billion a year.[8]

- As a leader, you pass on your leadership legacy. New leaders emulate the practices of their best bosses.

- The best way to retain your good people is to have positive and productive relationships with them.

- People who are positive have been shown to live longer.[9]

- Job satisfaction is a better predictor of longevity than smoking or exercise habits.[10]

The higher up you are in an organization, the more Emotional Intelligence, versus intelligence or technical expertise, determines your leadership success, contributing as much as 85-90 percent.

As a leader, you pass on your leadership legacy. New leaders emulate the practices of their best bosses.

CONSEQUENCES OF NOT RAISING YOUR EI

- The reasons for losing customers and clients are 70 percent EI related.[11]

- Fifty percent of time wasted in business is due to lack of trust, an EI competency.[12]

- Characteristics of executives who do poorly include lack of impulse control and the inability to work on teams, both addressed by EI competencies.[13]

- The cost to replace a management or sales position is 250 percent of the compensation package.[14]

The cost to replace a management or sales position is 250 percent of the compensation package.

THE 10 LEADERSHIP KEYS

L *eadership Keys* consists of a set of 11 cards. The first is a simple overview. It is followed by the 10 featured Leadership Keys. The following chart will help you see the relationship between the tool and the EI competency it supports.

TOOLS	COMPETENCY
#1. Leadership Two-Step	Leadership, Influence, Initiative
#2. Delegation	Developing Others
#3. Giving Feedback	Communication
#4. Coaching for Performance	Teamwork and Collaboration, Developing Others
#5. Assumption Ladder	Confidence, Decision Making
#6. Assumption Ladder Applications	Communication, Conflict
#7. Emotional Audit	Self-Awareness, Self-Management
#8. Tell, Sell, Test	Teamwork and Collaboration, Level of Involvement
#9. Managing Up and Partnering	Relationship Management, Building Bonds
#10. White Space Issues	Communication, Influence

#1. LEADERSHIP TWO-STEP

WHEN TO USE

Use as a guide to help you determine when to step in or out of a project. It is a great way to hold accountability and recognize and solve problems.

UNLOCKING THE KEY

Leadership has a rhythm and beat to it. You have to know the right time to *step in* and when to *step out*. Star leaders feel the beat and make the appropriate steps. They don't take on their direct reports' problems or "monkeys," but help them deal with their "monkeys" with support and resources. (The "monkeys" are the tasks that your direct reports have as deliverables. If they are lucky, you may suggest taking on their task because you have done it before, you can do it quicker, or you are too accommodating. They leave with one less task to do and you turn around to put their monkey down and see you are surrounded by your monkeys and everyone else's you so kindly took.)

Each step in or out reinforces the next step. When you do a good job in the initial step in, it becomes easier to step out. If you have been out for a while, when you step in for the second time it is appreciated by your direct reports.

Often leaders fail to step in when things are going well. They think they aren't necessary when things are running smoothly. To be a star it is important to not only solve problems, but also recognize and acknowledge the good efforts of your team and codify the practices to be repeated regularly.

KEY EXAMPLES

A CFO described a meeting she had delegated and quickly surmised, "It was going south, fast." She added, "I knew it was time to become a part of that meeting to get it on track." I was impressed how quickly she read the situation, felt the beat, and stepped in to "right the ship" at just the right time. Another executive who used the Leadership Two-Step Key as an assessment confessed that he rarely stepped out. "I actually have to go on vacation to step out." His goal is to better delegate, empower, and train his direct reports so that he doesn't have to be on-call at all times.

PRACTICING THE KEY
FOR YOURSELF

Rank yourself on each of the steps, on a 1–10 scale with 10 being the highest score. Practice the steps where you scored the lowest. Make sure you keep the Key out on your desk as a reminder.

FOR YOUR TEAM

Have each person rank themselves on each of the steps. Then ask:

- Which step had the highest score for you? Make sure you ask everyone where they scored the highest to get a tangible idea of their effectiveness.

- Which step had the lowest score for you? Make sure you ask everyone where they scored the lowest to get a tangible idea of their weak areas.

- If they had to improve one step, which one would it be and how would they do it?

- Create a list of best practices collected from people who score the highest and are the most successful with each of the Leadership Two-Steps. Copy and share it with the team.

Read through each of the steps and have people rate on a 1–10 scale how successful they are with each step.

LEADERSHIP TWO-STEP TOOL

1. **STEP IN:** Set the vision, systems, and structure; clarify expectations; identify the deliverables and timetable; establish resources available; encourage and motivate.

2. **STEP OUT:** Leave alone and let them come to you if they have questions; empower; encourage them to use their own best judgment; redirect to others; manage resources; fight urge to step in and take over; recognize and support; don't take on their problems or "monkeys."

1. **STEP IN:**

   A. **IF IT'S GOING WELL:** Support and acknowledge, spread the news, codify what is working well to replicate; hold the accountability; monitor, evaluate, and adjust; reiterate the vision and deliverables.

   B. **IF IT'S NOT GOING WELL:** "Right the ship"; understand what is the issue and what have they tried; make a decision quickly after you have checked in with them; reiterate the vision and deliverables; clarify expectations and resources.

2. **STEP OUT:** Leave alone and let them come to you if they have questions; empower; encourage them to use their own best judgment; redirect to others; manage resources; fight urge to step in and take over; recognize and support; don't take on their problems or "monkeys."

Repeat steps as needed.

#2. DELEGATION

WHEN TO USE

Use as a checklist any time you are delegating to make sure you hit all the important points.

UNLOCKING THE KEY

Star Performers excel at and practice delegation on a daily basis. The following model, adapted from Covey's Win-Win Agreements, has five steps that ensure your delegations are clear, empowering, and effective. Make sure they are performed sequentially and in-depth.

The "Recommend and then Act" and "Act and Advise" part of the guidelines can be used as a separate *check-in strategy*. Have both you and your direct reports fill out what they need to come to you with first for a recommendation before acting on it. With these, you have to give them the green light *(Recommend and then Act)*. Then, fill in what they are empowered to do and just inform you on *(Act and Advise)*. The resulting conversation can be very clarifying and can ensure that your direct reports are empowered and checking in with you appropriately.

KEY EXAMPLES

Leaders often complain that their direct reports are not taking enough initiative or they are disappointed that their direct reports have made decisions they wish they had known about ahead of time. If this rings true, ask yourself: "Have I told my direct reports what they can and cannot do?" Usually this conversation has not happened. (By the way, activating this micro-initiative can make you a star and separate you from the average performers.)

"Have I told my direct reports what they can and cannot do?"

Employees want to know how they are contributing to the bigger picture, and the impacts of their actions give them that kind of effective feedback. Usually impacts don't get talked about. Positive impacts give you the chance to tie in the value of their actions to the greater cause. An example of a negative impact may be: "If you don't get this done on time, it will slow down the production line and cost the company money. Plus, you and I will be to blame and that won't work for what we are trying to accomplish. Come to me if you need more support or resources."

KEY PRACTICES

FOR YOURSELF

Rank yourself on each of the delegation steps, on a 1–10 scale. Practice the steps that will help you the most to become great at delegation.

- Keep the Key out on your desk as a reminder.

- Try out the delegation steps when you next delegate.

- Get feedback on how the delegation went.

- Ask if there is a way you could be clearer in the next delegation.

- Encourage your direct reports to use the delegation steps when they delegate to others.

CHECK BACK CRITERIA

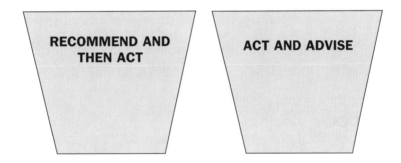

RECOMMEND AND THEN ACT

ACT AND ADVISE

FOR YOUR TEAM

Have each of your direct reports prepare "Check Back Criteria" with you and you do the same for them. What is in the *Recommend and then Act* bucket (examples include: changes to procedures, changes to an order, spending more than X, taking more time than X, hiring, firing, and personnel issues)?

What is in the *Act and Advise* bucket (examples include: standard procedures, daily operations, routine employee tasks, such as vacations, time cards, expenses with the budget)?

- Hold a conversation with each direct report. Have them share what they think is in their *Recommend and then Act* and *Act and Advise* buckets.

Hold a conversation with each direct report. Have them share what they think is in their Recommend and then Act *and* Act and Advise *buckets.*

- Try to hear them fully and negotiate what task should be in which bucket.

- Review your *Recommend and then Act* and *Act and Advise* regularly as things change and you develop more trust in their abilities.

- Encourage your direct reports to have this same "Check Back Criteria" conversation with their direct reports.

Change your style of speech to match the person you are delegating to. Some need a lot of information and assurance, while others just want the outline of the objective and need room to run with it.

REMEMBER

Your people want you to be clear, concise, and specific so that they can be successful.

Change your style of speech to match the person you are delegating to. Some need a lot of information and assurance, while others just want the outline of the objective and need room to run with it.

Give them stretch goals to challenge them. You want to get to where most of what they do is in the *Act and Advise* category.

Identify if there are specific occasions where they can *Act and Advise* but advise immediately, such as solving a crisis or customer complaint.

DELEGATION TOOL

1. DESIRED RESULTS: The big picture, beginning with the end in mind.

- What are you trying to accomplish?

- What are the key goals or deliverables?

- What kind of relationship do you want with your direct reports?

2. GUIDELINES: More specifics, how to get it done.

- Key dos and don'ts.

- At what point should they check in with you?

- Don't spend more than X amount of time or money.

LEVELS OF INITIATIVE: When to Check Back

RECOMMEND AND THEN ACT:

> **For example:** Personnel issues or changes that affect the project, budget, or timeline.

ACT AND ADVISE:

> People are empowered to make their own decisions and keep you informed periodically or immediately.

> **For example:** Daily routines with clarification of the amount of money, time, and resources they can use.

3. RESOURCES: What people, time, money, training, software, consultants, etc., can be used to achieve the desired result?

4. ACCOUNTABILITIES:

- What metrics do you have to measure the desired results?

- How will you know if they are being successful or not?

- When and where will they be measured?

- Others also act as accountabilities (e.g., executive feedback).

5. IMPACTS: What are the positive impacts on you, the team, and the individual from achieving the desired results?

> **For example:** More challenging projects, better leadership, eligible for more training, making budget, quality products, helping the team, more respect, and progress in their career goals.

NEGATIVE IMPACTS: The opposite of the positive ones given above. It's better to talk about them before negative consequences happen.

#3. GIVING FEEDBACK

WHEN TO USE

Use any time you need to give performance feedback, both positive and negative, to an employee, co-worker, or anyone else.

UNLOCKING THE KEY

Like delegation and coaching, giving feedback is another skill that can greatly enhance performance when both delivered and received well. The following model with the acronym SSBIR is adapted from the Center for Creative Leadership. This model can help in giving effective feedback. The goal of the feedback is for the person to both receive and use it. Before you learn how to give feedback it is important to ask yourself and answer some of the following questions. The effectiveness of your feedback session is based on your willingness to be honest with yourself first. Ask:

...giving feedback is another skill that can greatly enhance performance when both delivered and received well.

- Does the individual want to hear the feedback?

- How honest can I be?

- Will I hurt the person's feelings?

- What if he or she gets defensive?

- Will there be retribution?

- What will the person do with the feedback?

- What if he or she doesn't hear it and the same things keep happening?

- Will this hinder our relationship?

- Is this worth my risk?

WHEN TO GIVE FEEDBACK

1. FREQUENTLY: This gives you the best chance to reinforce positive behavior and influence changes in acceptable behavior. It makes it easier to focus on a specific behavior. So that your people don't only think feedback is negative, you should surprise them as much as you can with positive feedback.

2. TIMELY: Speak to employees when the experience is fresh. Don't give feedback only on exceptionally positive or negative things. Remember to give feedback when they are approaching the goal, not only when they have reached the goal.

3. OPPORTUNITY FOR DEVELOPMENT: Make employees aware of potential opportunities and provide steps for them to achieve their goals.

4. TO SOLVE PERFORMANCE PROBLEMS: Regular and frequent feedback puts money in the "emotional bank account" between people. It also makes it easier to be direct on a performance problem. When trust and respect have been built, it is easier to make a "withdrawal" from the account.

KEY EXAMPLES

STEP ONE: SET THE STAGE

This step gives listeners an opportunity to get ready to hear the feedback. Or they may say that now is not a good time. If they are ready, they will be less reactive. This is usually just one sentence. If the timing doesn't work for them, ask them to specify when it will work.

STEP TWO: STATE THE SITUATION

The second step anchors what you are specifically talking about. It is the "what," "where," or "when."

STEP THREE: STATE THE BEHAVIOR WITHOUT INTERPRETATIONS

This third step is very challenging. It helps if you write out what you will say before you give the feedback. You want to have it stated as a videotape would capture it. You do not want them to say, "No, I didn't," in response; instead, the behavior should be irrefutable.

HERE ARE SOME BAD EXAMPLES OF HOW TO GIVE FEEDBACK ABOUT SOMEONE'S BEHAVIOR:

- "Your attitude has gotten worse."
  They could say, "No it hasn't."
- "Your work is sloppy."
  They could say, "No it isn't."
- "I don't think you are putting your all into it."
  They could say, "Yes I am."

The feedback is subjective and not clear or solid.

HERE ARE SOME GOOD EXAMPLES FOR FEEDBACK ABOUT SOMEONE'S BEHAVIOR:

- "In the meeting today you raised your voice and were pointing fingers at people."

- "The customer reports that you were acting rudely and were slow in responding to her."

- "You told me that you would let me know if you were going to be late with the project and you never mentioned it."

The recipients could still try to deny these, but their ground would be less stable as you are reporting facts rather than interpretations.

STEP FOUR: STATE THE IMPACT

This is the most important step. Ideally you should have three or four impacts. The more impacts the better. This is your leverage to demonstrate all the people or situations, time, and money that have been impacted.

Ideally you should have three or four impacts.

- "The customer was disappointed…"

- "Others on the team were angry…"

- "This is a poor reflection on you, because…"

- "Waiting for you to arrive has cost us hundreds of dollars in wasted time."

- "We won't see the impact of this mistake immediately, but six months from now, when we go to renew the order, the customer may not want to do business with us again."

STEP FIVE: <u>RESOLUTION</u>

This last step starts with a quiz.

- "What thoughts do you have on how this can be resolved?"

- "How can we prevent this from happening again?"

If they have accepted the feedback, they will be able to give you some ideas of how to prevent these behaviors in the future. If they have *NOT* accepted the feedback, you will have to be more assertive and tell them what you want to see them do instead.

PRACTICING THE KEY

Take a few moments to write down your notes before giving feedback. This micro-initiative will increase your chances of others actually hearing the feedback and they will be less defensive in the process.

FOR YOURSELF

- How would you rate how well you give feedback?

- Keep the Key out on your desk as a reminder.

- Practice the SSBIR model and ask for feedback on how well you communicated.

FOR YOUR TEAM

- Teach the feedback model to your team and practice giving feedback using real-life scenarios. Discuss which statements seemed to best hit the mark.

- You can also use the Sample Feedback scenarios below to practice with your team.

REMEMBER

- If it is important, make an appointment to give the feedback.

- Be sensitive to the power imbalance (i.e., doing it in your office versus a neutral ground).

- Keep it simple.

- Leverage their strengths.

- Prepare the feedback to fit the learning style.

- Offer suggestions and support.

- Get their input about the feedback.

GIVING FEEDBACK TOOL, SSBIR

SET THE STAGE: INTENTION/READINESS TO LISTEN

- "I'd like to talk to you about something. Will this time work?"

- "My intention is to help you develop."

- "Can I give you some feedback?"

STATE THE SITUATION: WHAT HAPPENED AND WHERE?

- "In the meeting today…"

- "When you spoke to…"

- "In the report you wrote…"

STATE THE BEHAVIOR: WHAT DID YOU SEE OR HEAR, WITHOUT INTERPRETATIONS?

- "When you came late to the meeting…"

- "When you said…"

- "Three people said…"

- "I saw two errors…"

- "When the report was late…"

STATE THE IMPACT: ON MULTIPLE STAKEHOLDERS AND TIME FRAMES

- "The customer was disappointed…"

- "Others on the team were angry…"

- "This is a poor reflection on you, because…"

- "The organization wondered if…"

- "We lost money and time…"

- "I was disappointed and embarrassed…"

- "My boss asked me what was happening and was concerned…"

<u>R</u>ESOLUTION: HOW WOULD YOU LIKE TO SEE THE SITUATION RESOLVED?

- "What thoughts do you have on how this can be resolved?"

- "How can we prevent this from happening again?"

- "Next time I'd like to see this happen…"

- "Instead, can you do…?"

FEEDBACK PRACTICE SCENARIOS

In order to practice these scenarios, have two people play the roles of the employee and the manager. Have the manager then give the employee feedback. The rest of the group are observers and assess if the manager hit all the feedback phases. What worked and what are ways they can improve? If your team is big you can have the team get in groups of three and have a manager, employee, and observer. The observer gives feedback to the manager also using the SSBIR feedback model. What worked and what are ways they can improve? Have them pick another scenario and rotate roles.

1. Sam has done an excellent job taking on personal development tasks along with his day-to-day work. His technical skills have been a benefit to the rest of the department. Individuals have asked for Sam by name when they want someone to assist them. Sam stays late whenever important deadlines approach.

2. Jim comes to your project meeting late and then has a side conversation with Mary, which disrupts the meeting more. When interacting with others, he doesn't listen well and is always promoting his own ideas, which irritates everyone. You have received complaints from others that Jim isn't a team player.

3. Elizabeth has received technical advice from others that she doesn't incorporate into her work. You have already talked to her once about this. Now you have received complaints that she is ignoring the wants from other departments and they feel she is condescending to them.

4. Bob committed to having a report to you on a certain day and did not have it finished by then. You, in turn, got delayed with your schedule to production and got chewed out for not delivering. This is the third time that Bob has oversold what he could accomplish and hasn't considered contingencies and external factors.

5. Mary is very sociable and friendly, but you have been told she has not completed some of her tasks. Others seem to be working harder than she is. One person has come to you and complains that Mary is not carrying her weight in the department and is throwing the schedule off for everyone.

#4. COACHING FOR PERFORMANCE

WHEN TO USE

Use this model when you want to develop an employee and you don't want to keep answering the same kind of questions. Use it when you think their questions are a training opportunity versus just giving them an answer.

UNLOCKING THE KEY

When coaching, it is crucial that you save your advice or feedback until the *end* of your session, after you have fully heard the person. Often people are not looking for expert advice, but instead want validation or acknowledgement for what they are already doing. When I ask leaders, "How long do you wait before answering questions from direct reports?" Often they laugh and say, "If I don't interrupt them, maybe I'll wait three or four seconds." Then I ask, "How long do you think this person thought about his or her issues before coming to you for an answer?" They usually respond, "Anywhere from one to three days."

Often people are not looking for expert advice, but instead want validation or acknowledgement for what they are already doing.

So I say, "What are the chances, with three or four seconds of thought, that you are going to be right?" and "What is the possible impact on the employee?"

Obviously the longer you understand the issue—what the direct report's thoughts are and what he or she has already tried—the more accurate you can be with your advice. When you race to advice, the impact on the direct report can be negative, from feeling insulted or devalued to not being heard. You also increase your chances of your advice **not** being used when you dive in with it way before you have fully heard the situation and what they have tried.

When you race to advice, the impact on the direct report can be negative, from feeling insulted or devalued to not being heard.

The value of not jumping to advice is:

- The employee feels heard and understood.

- You will have more time to truly think.

- The employee can feel acknowledged and honored for the problem-solving he or she has already completed.

- You have an opportunity to see how your direct report thinks and problem-solves.

- Your employee can demonstrate his or her strengths to you.

- If placed at the end, your answer or advice has a better chance of being helpful and accepted.

KEY EXAMPLES

An assistant sits outside the executive's office all day long and interrupts her with questions that she begrudgingly answers. When asked why the assistant didn't try to get the answers on his own he replies, "Why should I? She knows all the answers." Many leaders have trained their direct reports to not think, as they feel obligated as the leader or manager to have all the answers.

Many leaders have trained their direct reports to not think...

One main goal of leaders is to create more leaders, to develop the "bench strength" in the organization. The easy and natural thing to do is to provide them all of the answers. But this doesn't always result in creating leadership! It is important to train or stretch employees to answer their own questions.

One executive I work with keeps this coaching tool on his desk and when an employee comes in with a question, the executive glances down at the tool and spends an extra few minutes going through each of the steps in his mind. This keeps him from jumping into advice! He finds that making a practice of asking what others think before he gives advice and answers is very effective. You can always say, "I'll give you my answer in a minute. Let me take an opportunity to see what you recommend as a way to help you develop."

PRACTICING THE KEY

FOR YOURSELF

- Try to hold your urge to be too helpful. Don't give advice immediately.

- Keep the Key out on your desk as a reminder.

- Practice listening fully, especially feeding back the content and feelings you heard.

- Ask for their recommendations before you give yours.

FOR YOUR TEAM

- Present the Coaching for Performance tool. Start by asking: "How long do you think about a response before responding to a direct report?"

- Ask them what the value is of not jumping to giving advice.

- Ask them what percentage of the time they look for validation versus advice.

- Use the coaching scenarios below.

COACHING FOR PERFORMANCE TOOL

STEP ONE: HEAR THE PROBLEM OR ISSUE FULLY

- What happened?

- When did it happen?

- Why do they think it occurred?

- Reflect back the content and emotions you have heard.

STEP TWO: GET MORE DETAILS

- Find out what they have tried.

- How long has it been going on?

- Who has been affected or impacted by the problem?

- What does anyone else think the problem is?

- Is there something that worked even part of the time?

- Reflect back the content and emotions you have heard.

STEP THREE: HONOR THEIR IDEAS FOR A SOLUTION

- If it is their problem, what do they think should be done next?

- What is the benefit of their idea?

- How long do they think it will take?

- What major obstacles do they see with this solution?

- What other resources will they need?

- How will they know if it's working or not?

- If there is more than one solution, ask about the merit of each.

- If they had to rank each answer, which is the highest, and why?

STEP FOUR: ASK IF THEY WANT YOUR FEEDBACK

- If not, just confirm what they will do.

- If you feel they really need it but don't want to hear it, offer it.

STEP FIVE: GIVE YOUR ADVICE OR FEEDBACK

- Don't just give the answer, but also use this as a *mentoring moment.*

- Make your thinking visible to them.

- What are your considerations for this choice?

- Why did you select this?

- What did you consider but rule out, and why?

- In a similar experience you might have had, what was the impact of that decision?

- How would you/have improved on it knowing what you know today?

- What things did they *not* consider with their choice (unintended consequences, impact on stakeholders, resources needed, time needed to implement it, skills needed)?

STEP SIX: PLAN

- What will be the next step?

- When should they check back with you?

- How will they know it is working?

COACHING PRACTICE SCENARIOS

Have two people play the roles of the employee and the manager. Have the manager then coach the employee. The employee will play the role of the employee described in the scenario and will have to ad-lib parts as the conversation gets into more depth than is presented in the scenario. The rest of the group are observers and assess if the manager hit all the coaching phases and if there is anything he or she could improve on.

If your team is big you can have the team get in groups of three and have a manager, employee, and observer. The observer gives feedback to the manager about their coaching using the Feedback model. What worked and what are ways they can improve? Have the triad pick another scenario and rotate roles.

1. Larry has been on your team for a year, and although very quiet and passive, is very technically sound. Larry doesn't speak up in meetings and agrees with the deadlines of the project without talking about any constraints he may have in meeting their needs.

   Other teams and team members are now upset with Larry and your team, as Larry has voiced additional needs and time to meet his deliverables. This came as a total surprise to them and the project will now miss one of its milestones. His lack of thinking about the big picture had been documented in his last review, and you talked to him about it then. You decide that now is the time to again talk to him about follow-through on promises and milestones he has committed to for your team.

2. Dana is one of your direct reports, and in her three years at your company has always been known as someone who aims to please. She joined your team six months ago, and she rarely gives you much pushback on deliverables or deadlines. She is often the first person to volunteer ideas or solutions to issues that come up in team meetings. While her can-do attitude is an asset in many situations, you've noticed that she is having trouble interacting with her fellow team members and motivating them to help meet upcoming deadlines. You've also

recently heard that some of her colleagues and team members feel she is "kissing up" to management. You have a regular weekly update meeting with Dana, and you decide to check in with her about her team interactions.

3. Stan has been a member of your team for about a year. He has been a strong performer, delivering good-quality work, and is liked by everyone. In his last review, you gave him feedback on areas for development, including deepening his subject matter expertise around some specific skills as well as suggesting he explore ways to more efficiently manage his time. (He is often late on delivery.) As a way to help him, you have asked for his weekly work plan. He said, "It is hard to give you that. You see, it is in my head and now everything will be pushed back if I have to write that down on paper..." He eventually agrees, but has not turned one in, and now three weeks have gone by.

Stan's workload has increased recently, and he has expressed frustration with being stretched too thin—unable to effectively manage his tasks, work on his professional development, and interact with the team. It was announced today that a project is going to shorten an upcoming deadline, which will directly increase Stan's workload even more. Stan has come into your office, clearly exasperated, unsure of how he can meet all of the demands on his time.

4. Jim has received his MBA recently and has been at your company for the last year. He was especially attracted to the company values when he signed on. So far he has worked on four projects and likes the work. You are his second boss only for the last two months. In his last review he received feedback that he didn't listen well to others and was always promoting his own ideas and could be argumentative in meetings.

You have noticed Jim to be very competitive and achievement-oriented. He is results-driven, always offering new ideas, taking responsibility for things that are many times outside his area and often challenging authority for the sake of innovation. Jim is very valuable to you and follows the values in his own way and is upset that others do not.

Jim has planned a meeting with you to talk about his career development. He highlighted his discontent and agenda topics in an email. They are:

• Others in the organization are not following the quality values, and when he does he is given a hard time for being too aggressive or taking too much time.

- He doesn't feel as empowered to question and change things as he thought he would, even by you.

- He doesn't feel trusted or respected by others, but instead feels incriminated for taking too much initiative.

- He doesn't feel like he has been oriented well to the job or had adequate reviews, support, feedback, or encouragement.

- He doesn't feel his talents are being used to do what he does best and is thinking this may not be the place for his career development.

- He doesn't feel motivated by you and thinks everyone is too busy to live the values and only gives them lip service.

- He expects to go through these points in the hope of receiving adequate advice that this is the place for him to pursue his career goals.

#5. ASSUMPTION LADDER
#6. ASSUMPTION LADDER APPLICATIONS

WHEN TO USE

Use when speaking to lay out your thinking to increase buy-in. Use when listening to walk someone down the Ladder to get a better idea at how they arrived at their conclusion(s). Also, the Ladder is good for unraveling conflicts and is an excellent team tool to enhance decision-making and communication. The Ladder is a universal EI tool. It helps with: Self-Awareness, Accurate Self-Assessment, Empathy, Service Orientation, Communication, Influence, Leadership, Conflict Management, Change Catalyst, Teamwork and Collaboration, and Developing Others.

UNLOCKING THE KEY

The Ladder is about your thinking process and how you arrive at and deliver your thoughts to others.

Communication is the mechanism to deliver your thoughts to others. The Ladder is about your thinking process and how you arrive at and deliver your thoughts to others. It is important to look at how you arrive at your thoughts and then to discover how you deliver them to others to be most effective.

MENTAL MODELS

It has been stated that we have as many as 60,000 thoughts a day. Ninety-five percent of those thoughts are the same ones we had yesterday. Why is that? The same thoughts keep recycling, and that is one reason why we use only 5–10 percent of our brainpower. These same or similar thoughts form patterns or clusters of our beliefs, yet leave out a plethora of other possible views. These become "mental models" or deeply ingrained assumptions, generalizations, or even pictures or images that influence how we understand the world and how we take action.

The mental models we carry around are usually *invisible* to us and others, yet are very powerful in their influence over our actions and responses to everything that occurs in our world. Often these mental models hold us prisoners to the "same old story" and prevent us from having the kind of open mind necessary to support new learning to help us grow and advance in our careers.

Leaders need to be explicit in their thinking. It is common to take shortcuts when you think and speak. But these shortcuts create confusion. People don't have the benefit of seeing your thinking process, what you focused in on, what you discounted, or what building blocks you crafted to support your thoughts and decisions. So isn't it natural that people may have a difficult time following your ideas or suggestions? Thus, our buy-in from others can be minimized.

KEY EXAMPLES

The Assumption Ladder is a modification of Chris Argyris's Ladder of Inference, introduced in Senge's *The Fifth Discipline*.[15] I have been using it in organizations for over 10 years with great success. When I return a year later and do follow-up assessments on the changes that have taken place, the Assumption Ladder is usually the tool that gets rave reviews. It has staying power because it is visual, makes sense to people, brings self-awareness to their thinking process, and helps in communicating their ideas.

People don't have the benefit of seeing your thinking process, what you focused in on, what you discounted, or what building blocks you crafted to support your thoughts and decisions.

The goal is to walk yourself and others up the Ladder. It allows everyone to lay out their thinking process and mental models. When you invite people up the Ladder, see if they agree with your data, selection of data, assumptions about the data, conclusions, and then the actions you suggest. If they know how you arrived, they may be more willing to go along with you. Or they may disagree, but it is more constructive to disagree with your selection of data and your assumptions than to argue with you about your conclusions.

Browsing through books in a bookstore provides a good example to illustrate walking up the Ladder. People often "thin-slice" or take a small piece of data and then make assumptions and generalize from that. Apparently, the average person picks up a book and spends about 8 seconds looking at the front cover and 15 seconds reading the back cover.[16] Portrayed on the Ladder, this process would look like:

DATA: The book is on the shelf with hundreds of others.

SELECTION OF DATA: The cover or spine speaks to you and you pick it up, spend 8 seconds on the front cover and 15 seconds reading the back cover.

ASSUMPTIONS:

- "This looks interesting and can help me in work."

- "The price may be too expensive for me; I wonder if I can get it used?"

- "The testimonials indicate that this book is very special and unique."

- "I always get books that I don't read; is this going to be another one?"

- "Maybe I should look at more of the book."

CONCLUSIONS: (Depending on which assumptions are followed.)

- You pick up the book and start opening up the pages and look at the table of contents for more data.

- Assumptions are validated as you see chapters and charts that are useful and you say, "Yes, I need this."

- You conclude that this book is not useful.

ACTIONS:

- You close the book and walk up to the checkout to buy it.

- You close the book and put it back on the rack.

PRACTICING THE KEY

It is a good idea to introduce the Ladder as a tool to enhance communication and understanding of others' viewpoints. To utilize the Ladder to its fullest, you, the leader, a facilitator, or another leader should bring the Ladder into your conversations. This person can be the "Ladder Carrier" and use terms that will help the team visualize the Ladder.

- "You are up on the Ladder on this one."

- "Can you make your thinking more visible?"

- "What are your assumptions in this decision?"

DOS AND DON'TS WHEN USING THE LADDER

DO	DON'T
Get people to hold your Ladder as you go up	Use the Ladder as a weapon
Open up for multiple viewpoints	Try to knock others off their Ladder
Invite others to challenge you	Get defensive
Practice walking up and down the Ladder	Expect this to be easy
Listen and inquire versus just advocating	Advocate without inquiry

SOME POINTERS

- Once a decision or conclusion is made, it becomes a force that looks for self-validation, and it is hard to entertain new data or ideas.

- The Ladder slows down the thinking process, and with more people commenting on the data and their assumptions you can get more creative and make more sound decisions. Your team can also help ensure quality decisions.

- If two people are at the top of their Ladders, you get debate and disagreement. If both people are low on the Ladder, you will get more of a dialogue before people are fixed to their positions and defending them.

- The Assumption Ladder Applications Tool gives you sentence stubs to walk up and down the Ladder. It is especially helpful when a direct report or client is at the top of the Ladder and you want to find out how he or she arrived there. It gives you an opportunity to insert a new selection of data, which opens up thinking and other viable possibilities.

Once a decision or conclusion is made, it becomes a force that looks for self-validation, and it is hard to entertain new data or ideas.

FOR YOURSELF

- Keep the Key out on your desk as a reminder.

- Look at the Ladder when you have to explain a decision to your team.

- Do your best to understand others' thinking by asking them questions that walk them down the Ladder.

FOR YOUR TEAM

- Introduce mental models and the Ladder to your team.

- Get copies of the Ladder for everyone to use and get a poster of the Ladder for your conference room or get everyone a set of the Leadership Keys.

- Pick a facilitator to help integrate the Ladder by inquiring which rung people are on and encouraging them to walk up the Ladder.

- Use the Ladder if there is a disagreement and see if the data and selection of data are the same. If so, go to the varying assumptions and locate where the disagreement lies.

Assumption Ladder

The goal is to make your thinking visible to others as you walk up the ladder.

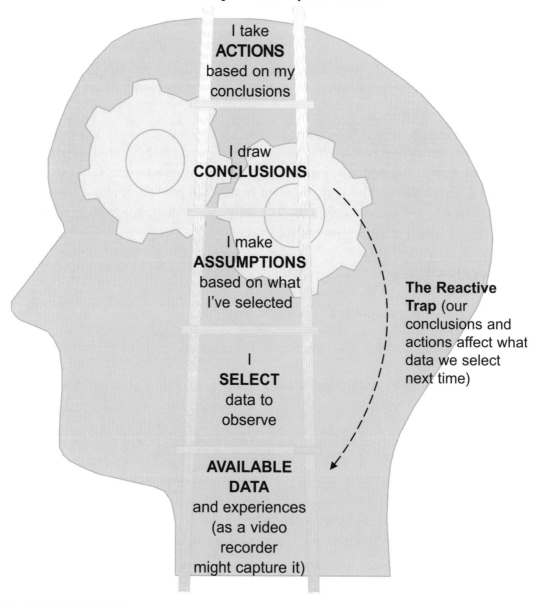

I take
ACTIONS
based on my
conclusions

I draw
CONCLUSIONS

I make
ASSUMPTIONS
based on what
I've selected

The Reactive Trap (our conclusions and actions affect what data we select next time)

I
SELECT
data to
observe

AVAILABLE DATA
and experiences
(as a video
recorder
might capture it)

Adapted from Luckner, J.L. and Nadler, R.S. *Processing the Experience.* Dubuque, Iowa: Kendall/Hunt Publishing Company, 1997.

Assumption Ladder Applications

**Below are some examples of sentences and sentence stubs
that will help you walk up or down the ladder.**

As a Listener:

I hear your actions.
What are they based on?
How did you arrive at these plans?

Tell me what conclusion you are drawing...
Could it be possible that...

Tell me what your assumptions are...
I'm curious, tell me more...
Is that the only way to look at it?

What piece are you looking at?
I see you're focusing on...
What is standing out to you from the data?

Give me all the facts...
What are all the findings?

ACTIONS

CONCLUSIONS

ASSUMPTIONS

SELECTED DATA

AVAILABLE DATA

As a Speaker:

Therefore, this is my plan...
These are steps I am taking...

It's obvious to me...
Therefore, I feel...
As a result...
To summarize...
Here we go again...

So, I'm assuming...
Here's what I attribute...
The next step for me is...

I am focusing on this piece...
Here's what I see happening...
Here's what I'm selecting...
This stands out to me...

Here are all the facts...
Here are all the findings...

Pay attention to intentions / Make your thinking visible

Adapted from Luckner, J.L. and Nadler, R.S. *Processing the Experience.*
Dubuque, Iowa: Kendall/Hunt Publishing Company, 1997.

#7. EMOTIONAL AUDIT

WHEN TO USE

Use whenever you are feeling frustrated, impatient, irritated, or other like emotions to help identify the problem and be more strategic in your actions.

UNLOCKING THE KEY

Lack of impulse control has been the undoing of many leaders (e.g., President Clinton, Dennis Kozlowski, Bernard Ebbers) and many corporate fraud examples. The Center for Creative Leadership lists the lack of impulse control as one of the main Executive Derailers.

Lack of impulse control has been the undoing of many leaders (e.g., President Clinton, Dennis Kozlowski, Bernard Ebbers) and many corporate fraud examples.

It is difficult to manage your emotions if you don't know what you are feeling. The Self-Awareness cluster of Emotional Intelligence is made up of Emotional Self-Awareness, Accurate Self-Assessment, and Confidence. All three of these are critical in development and are the foundation for raising other competencies. Goleman has stated that the Self-Awareness cluster should be developed first so as to facilitate the development of the other competencies.[17]

The first three questions of the Emotional Audit, "What am I thinking?" "What am I feeling?" and "What do I want?" are designed to highlight your self-awareness of what is actually going on for you in that moment. They help elucidate what may be behind the "closed door," although with focus these can become apparent. The goal is to become aware of what may have been a hidden or an automatic response. "What do I want now?" helps identify your intention of what you are trying to accomplish in this situation.

What are your automatic responses to your state that may be hindering you from achieving your desired intent?

The fourth question, "How am I getting in my way?" helps you establish your patterns or reactions to your emotional and cognitive state. What are your automatic responses to your state that may be hindering you from achieving your desired intent? Some of these may initially be blind spots, but with the time and assistance of a coach, boss, or co-worker you may "see" these patterns more clearly and then be able to "catch yourself" and "redirect your actions." The last question, "What do I need to do differently now?" is the strategic question that gives you more choice and allows your actions to better fit your intentions.

To understand your emotions and better manage them, use these questions frequently, especially when you feel yourself getting upset or frustrated, or if your triggers are getting activated. Wait five seconds until you get an answer to each question. Waiting allows some awareness of your answers to emerge.

KEY EXAMPLES

Mike was an executive who was getting irritated a lot, especially in meetings, where he felt he was wasting his time. In one meeting he got so hot and upset about a new procedure that he threw his briefcase across the room and swore at everyone in the room, including his boss. Let's look at his Emotional Audit. Here are Mike's answers:

1. WHAT AM I THINKING?

"This change makes no sense and will cost me more time doing more bureaucratic _____ (expletive) versus real work. I can't believe how dumb this is!"

2. WHAT AM I FEELING?

Frustrated, angry, and helpless.

3. WHAT DO I WANT NOW?

I want to be able to do my job unencumbered. I want to tell everyone that I don't agree with this and we shouldn't do it.

4. HOW AM I GETTING IN MY WAY?

My anger is preventing them from really hearing my point of view. I am scaring some of them. They see me as out of control and are not listening.

5. WHAT DO I NEED TO DO DIFFERENTLY NOW?

Take some deep breaths, relax, and address this concern with my boss outside of the meeting. This meeting is not the best place to address my concerns right now.

One key goal for Mike and other executives who have a lack of impulse control is to spend some time with a coach or their boss identifying their triggers and then preparing for meetings or other trigger situations until they feel they can catch themselves before they get too hot.

PRACTICING THE KEY

FOR YOURSELF

- Keep the Key out on your desk for easy reference.

- Try to catch yourself and your patterns and redirect your actions more quickly each time.

- Identify your key triggers with a coach or your boss.

- Use the Emotional Audit throughout the day.

FOR YOUR TEAM

- Have each person identify their key triggers.

- Brainstorm practices people use to successfully manage their emotions and redirect their focus.

- Encourage people to spend time every day going through the Emotional Audit.

EMOTIONAL AUDIT TOOL

1. What am I thinking?

2. What am I feeling?

3. What do I want now?

4. How am I getting in my way?

5. What do I need to do differently now?

#8. TELL, SELL, TEST

WHEN TO USE

Use when deciding how much input and involvement you want from your team. It will help you determine the style of leadership you should take.

UNLOCKING THE KEY

The sequence for using this Key was introduced by Peter Senge and others in their book *The Fifth Discipline Fieldbook,* and the model below has been adapted from that.[18] Different styles are appropriate at different times. Leaders also have styles that they are more comfortable with. Your team will be more involved and empowered the further down you go on the list.

TELL: This is a direction or order from you, the boss. There is no alternative and the team doesn't have a say.

- *You've* been told to do it.

- There's no time for another solution.

SELL: Here you are encouraging and persuading the audience to do something. You are giving them all the reasons and benefits. There is no alternative and the team doesn't have a say, although you need their compliance.

- You have made up your mind.

- You need buy-in from others to get it done.

TEST: As the leader, you have a good idea of what you want to see happen, but you want to get input and involvement from others before proceeding. The team has a limited voice and you still hold the veto power.

- You know about 70 percent of the solution.

- You want validation and input.

- You'd like feedback before you decide.

CONSULT: As the leader, you have an idea of what you want to see happen but need more input from others before taking action. Your team may have subject experts who know more than you do on specific topics. You still hold the veto power.

- You have a 30 percent idea of the result.

- You think there is some good information that can be gained.

CO-CREATE: The leader here is equal with the other team members regarding the specific topic. You need their expertise to put together the solution. The team is fully empowered.

- You have been told what to get but don't know how to get there.

- You have expertise and resources in the team to reach the goal.

KEY EXAMPLES

Below are appropriate times to use these leadership styles:

TELL: There is a crisis or emergency; time is of the essence; you were told by your boss, the board, or shareholders.

SELL: There has been an acquisition or merger, or a new product is being introduced. You want to get people's buy-in to this new event.

TEST: The quality of your decision needs to be checked before it goes out. It could be a presentation to a board or investors with your feedback.

CONSULT: This may be a decision about recognition, where to hold an event, and what kind of food to get. As the leader, you will take all these ideas in advisement and make the decision.

CO-CREATE: Decide on the team values or visions. Your input is equal to everyone else's.

PRACTICING THE KEY

FOR YOURSELF

- Keep the Key out on your desk for easy reference.

- Decide which style is your most comfortable.

- Which style are you least comfortable with?

- Which style should you practice the most?

FOR YOUR TEAM

- Discuss which styles they are most comfortable with and least comfortable with.

- Decide what level of involvement is needed by each decision.

TELL, SELL, TEST TOOL

LEADERSHIP	WHEN TO USE	STYLE
TELL	You've been told to do it. There's no time for another solution.	"Here's what I want us to do." "This time there is no choice."
SELL	You've made up your mind. You still need buy-in to get it done.	"Here's my idea."
TEST	You know about 70 percent. You want validation and input. You'd like feedback before you decide.	"I'm thinking this." "Do you think this will work?" "What am I missing?"
CONSULT	You have a 30 percent idea of the result. You think there's some more good information that could be gained.	"This is what I want it to end up like." "What are your ideas to make this work?"
CO-CREATE	You've been told what to get. You don't know how to get there. You have expertise and resources in the team.	"This is where we need to go." "I don't have the answer." "I need your help." "What do you think?"

From *The Fifth Discipline Fieldbook* by Peter M. Senge, Charlotte Roberts et al, copyright 1994 by Peter M. Senge, Charlotte Roberts, Richard B. Ross, Bryan J. Smith and Art Kleiner. Used by permission of Doubleday, a division of Random House.

#9. MANAGING UP AND PARTNERING

WHEN TO USE

When dealing with a key stakeholder like your boss or partner (where you are equals) and you want to improve your collaboration process.

UNLOCKING THE KEY

When dealing with your supervisor or key customer, stakeholder, or partner, it is important to understand their preferences and needs. This will help you align your performance to be viewed as a star by them. Below are questions and conversations to assist you. Each of these points is usually not done by the average performer. To be a Star Performer, spending some time thinking about these and initiating conversations on these points will lead to your top performance.

RESPONSIBILITY ALIGNMENT: What do your supervisors or partners see as the top five responsibilities of your position? What do you see as the top five responsibilities of your position? Typically only 1.5 of the five responsibilities are the same, therefore you may be working on the wrong priorities. This conversation will help you work on the areas that will get you the furthest in your supervisors' or partners' eyes.

EXPECTATIONS CLARIFICATION: What are your supervisors' or partners' key expectations of you? Ask them: "For this relationship to be a success, what are the key things I need to do and not do?" Make sure you talk about responsiveness on email and voice mail.

INFORMATION GATHERING: Do they like a formal approach or informal? Should you come with reports, data, agendas, and be highly organized? Or can you be more informal and talk about the big-picture possibilities and opportunities. Mirror their language; are they visual ("see, view") or auditory ("sounds like, talk, resonate") or kinesthetic ("get a hold of, action").

DECISION STYLE: How do your supervisors or partners make decisions? Is it quickly with limited data? Or is it deliberate with a lot of information. Do they like to discuss all the possibilities? Or should you leave the office and let them reflect on it and get back with them in a day? If you are not sure, ask them.

CONFLICT STYLE: Do they thrive in conflict or avoid it? Do you feel each conversation is part of the debating club? Or do they strive for harmony and peace at all costs? If you are not sure, ask them.

KEY EXAMPLES

An executive I was working with was newly promoted to a management position. The culture was fast-paced and she was encouraged to get in there and "just do it" without any formal orientation or training. This was difficult because she wanted more clarity of what she could and couldn't do. As a result, she wasn't just getting in there and doing it. Attempts to schedule time with her boss kept getting cancelled or rescheduled. This was becoming frustrating for her.

Instead of waiting for the clarity to come from above, she decided to be proactive and developed her answers to the questions above. She watched her boss and superiors in meetings and used the walk time between meetings to get "just-in-time mentoring" and get her questions answered. She then developed her list of the Check Back Criteria, mentioned in the Delegation Tool above, and shared that with her boss when there was a spare moment before a meeting started, rather than waiting for a formal meeting.

With her own initiative, the executive got the answers she was waiting for and was better able to just "go for it."

PRACTICING THE KEY

FOR YOURSELF

- Keep the Key out on your desk for easy reference.

- Answer all the questions above that you can on your own.

- Schedule time with your boss or partner and go through the questions and your answers with an introduction of wanting to clarify and improve your relationship with them.

FOR YOUR TEAM

- Hold a meeting and go over the "best boss" relationship they have had. What did this boss do and say and what was the impact on them? Write it on a flip chart. For yourself, make a point of clarifying and get feedback on some of the areas that you could do better for them.

- Looking at the lists, what are two things that each person could do more of to improve their relationship with their boss and with the people who report to them?

- Have a discussion about the "best partnership" relationship they have had. Again, what made this the best? What did they do and what did their partner do?

- Looking at the lists, what are two things that each person could do more of to improve their relationship with a partner.

#10. WHITE SPACE ISSUES

WHEN TO USE

Use when speaking to your team or the company about a change initiative or a sales event.

UNLOCKING THE KEY

The word *intelligence* comes from a Latin derivation meaning "entering through the lines." People are always using their intelligence to enter or read into the lines of what you are saying or not saying. They fill in the white spaces between your words almost automatically, because it gives them a sense of understanding, control, or security. In the caveman days, gossip served a similar function. It was information that gave tribes the sense of understanding the meaning of things. They could "connect the dots," which helped their survival.

Today, gossip or "making stories" serves a similar purpose. Whether you like it or not, people will always put a personal spin on everything you say, and they do it almost instantaneously. Are their interpretations positive, accurate, or constructive? Probably not! Here is an illustration of what usually happens when you speak and others "listen."

KEY EXAMPLES

An Executive says about a possible acquisition:

- *"We are looking into all kinds of possibilities that will help us maintain our viability and profitability."*

How people fill in the white space:

- *"I didn't think we were in such trouble. This may be worse than I thought. I wonder if I should start looking elsewhere."*

- *"If we are looking to purchase another company, that means there will be layoffs and my job could be in jeopardy."*

- *"Oh no, with this going on in the executive office, they will never have time to focus on my project. This is going to hurt my career advancement."*

If you don't fill in the white space, your people will, and you will be reacting to all the misinterpretation.

Here is how you can fill in the white space with what is positive, accurate, and constructive:

An Executive says about a possible acquisition:

"We are looking into all kinds of possibilities that will help us maintain our viability and profitability. Right now there are a few exciting opportunities. Now, because of due diligence, I can't tell you exactly what. But what I can tell you about is our process. We have a small team of seasoned executives who are looking at all the facts. This will be a well-thought-out and informed decision. Our criteria in the decision are:

> *"First, that we don't interrupt our day-to-day business and focus.*
>
> *"Second, that we keep all the talent here.*
>
> *"Third, we want this to be growth for you and the company. We want you to be a part of any changes that go on.*
>
> *"We plan to have a monthly lunch meeting to answer your questions and keep you informed. Contact me or my office if you have questions."*

If you can respond to the "unasked questions," you build credibility and security. People won't have to "create their own stories" as much.

In this scenario, the leader tries to fill in the white space to the best of his or her ability, answering many of the questions people may have. If you can respond to the "unasked questions," you build credibility and security. People won't have to "create their own stories" as much.

KEY PRACTICES

FOR YOURSELF

- Keep the Key out on your desk for easy reference.

- Challenge yourself and others on some of their assumptions as you and they fill in the white space.

- Remember, white space is going to get filled in by others anyway. You can be preventative and informing by telling your people what you know.

- Use the term *white space* so it remains a viable image and concept for your team.

FOR YOUR TEAM

- Explain to your staff how filling in white space is natural and how you want them to become conscious of how they are doing it.

- Ask, "What are the ways you can become more aware of how you and others fill in the white space?"

- Constantly ask for feedback about your communications. Ask, "What did you hear?" Then re-clarify.

- Ask your team to let you know if they are not hearing enough from you and are beginning to fill in white space negatively.

- Evaluate if their interpretations are Positive, Accurate, and Constructive. This is called a PAC interpretation. If what you read or hear is not accurate and constructive, make sure you clarify.

WHITE SPACE TOOL

The following visual will help you see and remember the process.

The bold line indicates what you said:

"██"

The minus or hyphen signs indicate what gets filled in quickly by others. Remember, they are entering through the lines to grasp what it seems you have said. Again, it is usually inaccurate and judgmental, and rarely gives you the benefit of the doubt.

— —

— —

— —

"██"

++

++

++

Positive signs indicate what you say when you proactively fill in the white space with accurate and positive data, talking about opportunities.

"██"

White space is always going to get filled in by others. You can plan ahead and inform your people of what you know and prevent too many misunderstandings.

GOOD LUCK IN YOUR JOURNEY TOWARD BETTER EMOTIONAL INTELLIGENCE AND STAR PERFORMANCE!

NOTES

1. C. Cherniss and D. Goleman, *The Emotionally Intelligent Workplace: How to Select for, Measure, and Improve Emotional Intelligence in Individuals, Groups, and Organizations* (San Francisco: Jossey-Bass, 2001).

2. Ibid.

3. D. Goleman, *Working with Emotional Intelligence* (New York: Bantam Books, 1998).

4. C. Cherniss and D. Goleman, *The Emotionally Intelligent Workplace: How to Select for, Measure, and Improve Emotional Intelligence in Individuals, Groups, and Organizations* (San Francisco: Jossey-Bass, 2001).

5. J. Zenger and J. Folkman, *The Extraordinary Leader* (New York: McGraw-Hill, 2002).

6. Ibid.

7. Hay Group, *Inventory of Leadership Styles and Organizational Climate:* Survey Certification material (Boston, MA: 2003).

8. *Gallup Management Journal*, "Positivity Increases Productivity" (July 8, 2004).

9. T. Rath and D.O. Clifton, *How Full Is Your Bucket?* (New York: Gallup Press, 2004).

10. Department of Labor, 1988.

11. Six Seconds website, 6seconds.org, 2004.

12. Ibid.

13. J.B. Leslie and E. Van Velsor, "A Look at Derailment Today: North America and Europe," Center for Creative Leadership (Greensboro, NC: 1996).

14. Center for Creative Leadership, ccl.org, 2003.

15. P. Senge, *The Fifth Discipline: The Art and Practice of the Learning Organization* (New York: Doubleday, 1990).

16. D. Poynter, *The Self-Publishing Manual* (Santa Barbara, CA: Para Publishing, 2002.)

17. D. Goleman, *Working with Emotional Intelligence* (New York: Bantam Books, 1998).

18. From *The Fifth Discipline Fieldbook* by Peter M. Senge, Charlotte Roberts et al, copyright 1994 by Peter M. Senge, Charlotte Roberts, Richard B. Ross, Bryan J. Smith and Art Kleiner. Used by permission of Doubleday, a division of Random House.

REFERENCES

Center for Creative Leadership, http://ccl.org, 2003.

Cherniss, C. and Goleman, D. *The Emotionally Intelligent Workplace: How to Select for, Measure, and Improve Emotional Intelligence in Individuals, Groups, and Organizations.* San Francisco: Jossey-Bass, 2001.

Department of Labor, 1988.

Gallup Management Journal, "Positivity Increases Productivity," July 8, 2004.

Goleman, D. *Working with Emotional Intelligence.* New York: Bantam Books, 1998.

Hay Group. *Inventory of Leadership Styles and Organizational Climate.* Survey Certification material. Boston, MA, 2003.

Leslie, J.B. and Van Velsor, E. "A Look at Derailment Today: North America and Europe," Center for Creative Leadership, Greensboro, NC, 1996.

Poynter, D. *The Self-Publishing Manual.* Santa Barbara, CA: Para Publishing, 2002.

Rath, T. and Clifton, D.O. *How Full Is Your Bucket?* New York: Gallup Press, 2004.

Senge, P. *The Fifth Discipline: The Art and Practice of the Learning Organization.* New York: Doubleday, 1990.

Senge, P.M., Roberts, C., Ross, R.B., Smith, B.J. and Kleiner, A. *The Fifth Discipline Fieldbook.* New York: Doubleday, 1994.

Six Seconds website, http://6seconds.org, 2004.

Zenger, J. and Folkman, J. *The Extraordinary Leader.* New York: McGraw-Hill, 2002.

RELDAN S. NADLER, Psy.D.

D r. Reldan S. Nadler is a world-class executive coach, leadership consultant, and team trainer. His clients include DreamWorks Animation, Anheuser-Busch, BMW, Comerica Bank, and Honda. He is a sought-after speaker and consultant specializing in the utilization of Emotional Intelligence (EI) tools and practices to enhance leadership performance. He has also authored the *Leaders' Playbook: How to Apply Emotional Intelligence—Keys to Great Leadership* and two best-selling books on leadership and team performance. Relly founded True North Leadership, Inc., an executive and organizational development firm. He lives in Santa Barbara, California, with his wife, Juli, and their two children, Dillon and McKensey.

HOW TO ENGAGE THE AUTHOR

Contact:
Relly Nadler, Psy.D.
True North Leadership, Inc.
1170 Camino Meleno
Santa Barbara, CA 93111
805-683-1066 Fax 805-692-6738
Rnadler@truenorthleadership.com

TO BRING EMOTIONAL INTELLIGENCE COMPETENCIES INTO YOUR ORGANIZATION

CONSULTING, COACHING, AND TRAINING SERVICES

- Keynotes and Presentations
- Multi-day Leadership Development training for your teams, based on Emotional Intelligence
- Executive coaching—senior leaders and emerging leaders
- 360-degree feedback
- Teambuilding training for executive teams and departments
- "Relly Tele"—telecourses to help in utilizing the tools
- Organizational consulting
- Organizational assessments
- Succession planning

Go to our website for more information on these services and to sign up for our mailing list: www.truenorthleadership.com.

For more information about the *Leadership Keys Field Guide* and bulk orders, contact *Psyccess Press,* a division of True North Leadership, Inc. 1170 Camino Meleno, Santa Barbara, CA 93111, 805-683-1066.

LEADERS' PLAYBOOK
HOW TO APPLY EMOTIONAL INTELLIGENCE—
KEYS TO GREAT LEADERSHIP

CLOSING THE GAP BETWEEN THE THEORY AND PRACTICE OF EMOTIONAL INTELLIGENCE

- *Interviews with Star Performers highlighting their Key Practices*
- *Coach's Corner and proven strategies used with executives*
- *EI Profiles of famous leaders and politicians*

100+ HANDS-ON STRATEGIES DEVOTED TO RAISING THE COMPETENCIES OF:

- Self-Confidence
- Teamwork and Collaboration
- Developing Others
- Communication and Empathy

TOOLS, STORIES, CHECKLISTS, ASSESSMENTS, AND STRATEGIES INCLUDING:

- EI Star profile™
- Hiring Checklist™
- Derailer Detector™
- Teambuilding activities
- Meeting Menace Checklist™
- 100 Leadership Check-In Questions and much more

Go to our website for more information on the product and prices and to sign up for our mailing list: www.truenorthleadership.com.

LEADERS' PLAYBOOK FIELD GUIDE

Designed for managers, leaders, and coaches to bring these tools and plays to their team, it is a complete *turn-key curriculum* for a team leader or coach. It includes:

CD AND NOTEBOOK

1. Powerpoint presentations with notes include:
- EI introduction with political and CEO profiles
- Mental models and Assumption Ladder presentation
- Communication Tools: Feedback, Delegation, and Coaching tools

2. PDFs of the Key Tools and checklists to distribute to your team
- EI Star Profile™
- Derailer Detector™
- Meeting Menace Checklist™
- Team meetings
- Guidelines for running a great meeting
- How to establish roles within a team meeting
- The Meeting Checklist™
- Teamwork Ingredients Survey™
- 100 Leadership Check-In Questions
- Hiring Checklist™
- Motivation Skills Matrix™
- Feedback Tool™
- Delegation Tool™
- Coaching for Performance Tool™
- Assumption Ladder™

3. Curriculum agendas for implementing the tools

4. More teambuilding activities that are not in the Playbook

Site licenses and affiliate programs available.

Go to our website for more information on the product and prices and to sign up for our mailing list: www.truenorthleadership.com.

WWW.TRUENORTHLEADERSHIP.COM